Carlo Acutis

Blessed Are the Righteous

1991–2006
Born in London, United Kingdom
Feast Day: October 12
Patron of young
computer programmers

"Blessed are they who hunger
and thirst for righteousness,
for they will be satisfied."
Matthew 5:6

Text by Barbara Yoffie
Illustrated by Chris Sharp

Dedication

To my family:
my parents Jim and Peg,
my husband Bill,
our son Sam and daughter-in-law Erin,
and our precious grandchildren
Ben, Lucas, and Andrew

To all the children I have had the privilege
of teaching throughout the years.

Imprimi Potest:
Kevin Zubel, CSsR, Provincial
Denver Province, the Redemptorists

Published by Liguori Publications, Liguori, Missouri 63057
To order, visit Liguori.org or call 800-325-9521.

ISBN (print): 978-0-7648-2880-5
ISBN (digital): 978-0-7648-7242-6

Liguori Publications, a nonprofit corporation, is an apostolate of the Redemptorists. To learn more about the Redemptorists, visit Redemptorists.com.

Printed in the United States of America
27 26 25 24 23 / 5 4 3 2 1
First Edition

Dear Parents and Teachers:

Saints and Me! is a six-set series of children's books about saints, including the holy people of the: *Saints of North America* who served our homeland; *Saints of Christmas*, who teach us to love Jesus; *Saints for Families*, who modeled God's love within and for the domestic Church; *Saints for Communities*, who served Jesus through various roles and professions; and *Saints for Sacraments*, who showed great love for the sacraments.

The eight books in *Saints of the Beatitudes* (a word meaning "a list of blessings from God") introduce nine holy people who exemplify attributes Jesus articulated in his Sermon on the Mount. Faustina Kowalska's diary *Divine Mercy in My Soul,* read by millions, helped spread God's message of mercy. Patrick, a missionary, brought Christianity to Ireland. Monica prayed her wayward son, Augustine, would return to the faith. He did and was canonized. Katharine Drexel abandoned her comfortable life to become a nun. Carlo Acutis shared his faith and love of the Eucharist through technology. Bernadette Soubirous experienced visions of the Blessed Virgin Mary. Pope John XXIII convoked the Second Vatican Council, hoping to revive the Church. Jude was an apostle of our Lord.

Which saint was captured by pirates and sold into slavery? Name the saints with back-to-back feast days (August 27–28). Who gave $20 million to build churches and schools? Who created a website about eucharistic miracles? Who did Jesus appear and speak to? Who said, "My job is to inform, not to convince"? Who wrote *Peace on Earth* in 1963? Who is the patron of impossible causes? Find out in the *Saints of the Beatitudes* set—part of the *Saints and Me!* series—and help children connect to the lives of the saints.

Introduce your children or students to *Saints and Me!* as they:

—**READ** about the lives of the saints and are inspired by their stories.

—**PRAY** to the saints for their intercession.

—**CELEBRATE** the saints and relate them to their lives.

Free activities for children to use with this book may be downloaded at Liguori.org.

The Beatitudes

Divine blessings Jesus names in his Sermon on the Mount

Matthew 5:3–12

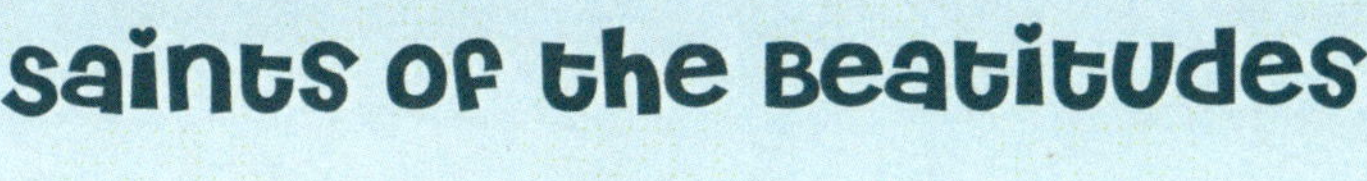

Saints of the Beatitudes

Patrick
Blessed Are the Poor in Spirit (Verse 3)

Monica and Augustine
Blessed Are the Mournful (Verse 4)

Katharine Drexel
Blessed Are the Meek (Verse 5)

Carlo Acutis
Blessed Are the Righteous (Verse 6)

Faustina Kowalska
Blessed Are the Merciful (Verse 7)

Bernadette
Blessed Are the Pure of Heart (Verse 8)

Pope John XXIII
Blessed Are the Peacemakers (Verse 9)

Jude the Apostle
Blessed Are the Persecuted (Verses 10–12)

God gave Saint Carlo Acutis wonderful gifts. Two gifts were a strong faith and a desire to do the right thing. Carlo knew faith and righteousness were special. He wanted to please God. He did this by growing in holiness, helping people in need, and encouraging everyone he met to love God.

Carlo was born in 1991, in London, United Kingdom. He was a cheerful baby with a big smile and dark eyes.

A few months after he was born, his family moved to Milan, Italy. It was a modern city, with old churches, large buildings, museums, and beautiful parks.

One morning, Carlo and his mother took a walk to the park near their home. On the way, they passed a beautiful church. "Mom, can we go inside? I want to say hello to Jesus," Carlo said.

"Of course, Carlo, but we must be very quiet," his mom answered. Inside, he knelt, closed his eyes, and said a prayer.

Carlo liked to pray and spend time in church. Sometimes he would put flowers by the statue of the Blessed Virgin Mary and smile at her. He loved Mary. And he loved to pray the rosary. The rosary was his favorite prayer!

As Carlo grew, so did his faith and his desire to do the right thing. He was filled with the love of God and often thought about what heaven would be like.

He received special permission to celebrate his first Communion when he was seven years old, a few years before his friends at school. He told his parents, "I want to go to Mass every day!"

"I feel close to Jesus," he said. "I wish everyone would go to Mass so they could feel close to Jesus, too!" Carlo also grew in faith and holiness at weekly confession. Talking to the priest helped him understand how he could follow Jesus and become more like him.

Carlo smiled a lot and was fun to be around. He helped classmates with their schoolwork. One student gave Carlo a high five and said, "Thanks, Carlo! Now I know how to do this math problem. You are the best!"

Carlo was kind to everyone. You could depend on him to stop a fight or stick up for a student who was being teased. Teasing is wrong, and Carlo wanted to do the right thing.

Carlo had many friends, but Jesus was his best friend. He spent time in eucharistic adoration almost every day. During this quiet prayer time, he talked and listened to Jesus and shared his thoughts. Carlo was such a good example that his parents started going to Mass more often. Some of his friends returned to church. He told them, “Let’s go to Mass first, and then play soccer.” Carlo loved soccer, but Jesus always came first.

Saint Francis of Assisi was one of Carlo's favorite saints. His family spent vacations in the town of Assisi, Italy. It was a special place for him. "Carlo is so happy here," his mother said.

Carlo was like Saint Francis in many ways. They both loved the Eucharist. They liked to live simply and cared for God's creation. On walks, Carlo picked up trash in the park, on the street, and at the beach!

Saint Francis and Carlo loved animals! Carlo had four dogs, two cats, and lots of goldfish. He enjoyed walking his dogs and playing games with them. He made silly movies with his pets and dressed them in costumes. His movies were funny and made his family and friends laugh.

Like most kids his age, Carlo enjoyed video games. But he was careful not to spend too much time playing them. He did not like to waste time. He balanced his days with family time, study, play, and prayer. He taught religion classes to younger students, worked in a soup kitchen, and used his allowance to buy food for the poor.

Carlo was interested in computer programming. He read books and taught himself to program, make videos, and create websites. “Your work is amazing. You are a computer genius,” his friends told him. He volunteered his time and helped start a web page for his school and parish.

At eleven, Carlo joined his love of Christ in the Eucharist with his computer skills and made a website about eucharistic miracles! Miracles are amazing events that can't be explained. Eucharistic miracles can help people believe the truth that Christ is really present in the Eucharist.

Carlo found over 100 eucharistic miracles. Then he put interesting stories and pictures on his website. He finished the project in two years.

"I am really excited to share my faith and love of the Eucharist by using technology," Carlo said. He hoped and prayed that people all over the world would visit his website. He wanted everyone to grow close to Jesus Christ.

In October 2006, Carlo learned he had leukemia, a serious blood disease. He died at the age of fifteen.

His short time on earth was filled with happy times with his family and friends. But most importantly, he shared his love of Christ in the Eucharist with millions of people around the world. Thanks to his website, he still does!

As the story of Carlo's holy life and witness spread, people prayed that he would be named a saint. His cause for canonization began in 2013. Just seven years later, on October 10, 2020, Pope Francis beatified him in Assisi, Italy. Despite the COVID-19 pandemic, many of Carlo's friends were present at the beatification Mass.

Carlo was canonized—officially named a saint—in 2025 by Pope Leo XIV. Today, Saint Carlo is an inspiration for all of us to keep Jesus Christ at the center of our lives.

God has a gift for every girl and boy.
He fills your heart with
kindness, love, and joy.

♥ ♥ ♥

Saint Carlo, Jesus was your best friend.
The Eucharist gave you hope and strength.
Help me to grow closer to Jesus.
Help me to be holy. Amen.

GLOSSARY (NEW WORDS)

Beatified: A person is named "Blessed" in a special Mass and is one step away from being canonized

Canonization: The formal process that results in declaring someone a saint

COVID-19 pandemic: A serious illness caused by a virus that spread all over the world and led people to make many changes in how they lived their daily lives

Eucharist: The sacrament in which bread and wine become the Body and Blood of Jesus Christ

Eucharistic Adoration: Spending time in a church or chapel, quietly praying to Jesus before the tabernacle or a monstrance

Eucharistic Miracles: These help people believe our Lord is present in the Eucharist. A miracle is an amazing event that cannot be explained.

Leukemia: A serious blood disease

Righteousness: The ability to do the right thing

Soup Kitchen: A place where food is prepared and given to poor people

Technology: The use of computers or software

Website: A place on the internet with information about a certain subject

Visit Saint Carlo Acutis' eucharistic miracles website:
miracolieucaristici.org

Saints and me!

SAINTS FOR SACRAMENTS

Booklets in this set were honored by the Association of Catholic Publishers!

John the Baptist:
Saint for Baptism
827969

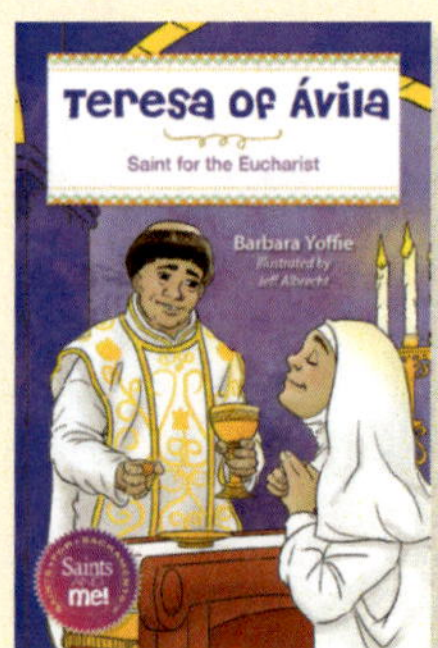

Teresa of Ávila:
Saint for the Eucharist
827938

Padre Pio:
Saint for Reconciliation
827921

Philip Neri:
Saint for Confirmation
827976

Maximilian Kolbe:
Saint for Anointing
of the Sick 827983

Louis and Zélie Martin:
Saints for Matrimony
827945

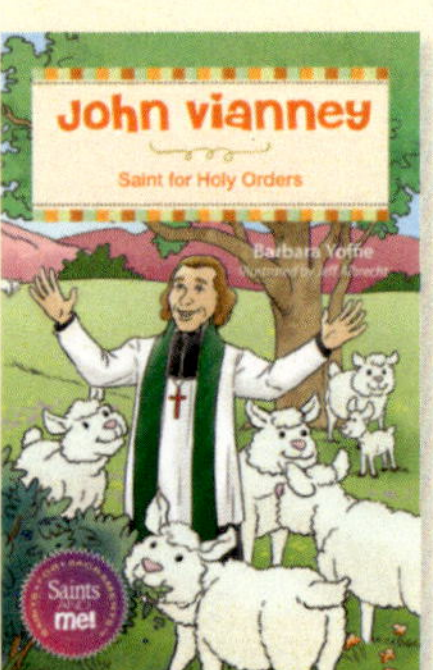

John Vianney:
Saint for Holy Orders
827952

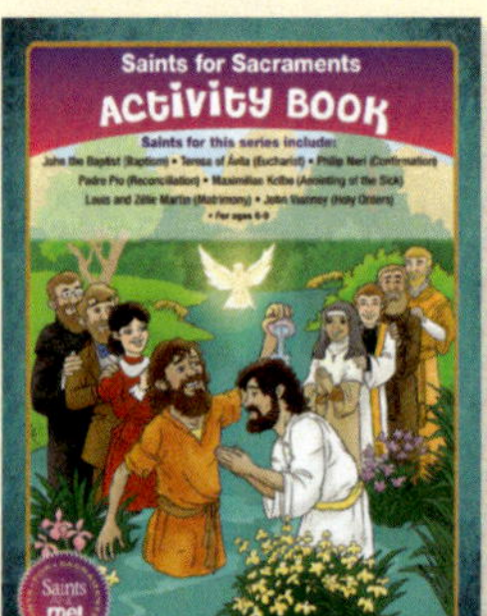

Saints for Sacraments
Activity Book 828010

Get the Complete Set!

Saints for Sacraments Collection A00085
(*Activity Book* sold separately)

Booklets: 32 pages, 5.5 x 8.5,
Full-color illustrations

Activity Book: 96 pages, 8.5 x 11

Order today! Call 800-325-9521 or visit Liguori.org.